HELPING CHILDREN COPE WITH DEATH

A Practical Resource Guide for *Someone Special Died*

By Joan Singleton Prestine

D1361410

Fearon Teacher Aids

A Paramount Communications Company

Editorial Director: Virginia L. Murphy

Editor: Carolea Williams

Copyeditor: Lisa Schwimmer

Cover and Inside Illustration: Virginia Kylberg

Design: Marek/Janci Design

Cover Design: Lucyna Green

Library of Congress Catalog Card Number: 93–72028

ISBN 0-86653-928-X
Printed in the United States of America
1. 9 8 7 6 5 4 3 2 1

Acknowledgments

I want to thank the following people for their support, encouragement, and expertise. Their suggestions were invaluable.

Doug Prestine, my husband, best friend, and computer expert

Ginger Murphy, editorial director and ego booster

Carolea Williams, editor and advisor

Lisa Schwimmer, copyeditor and good listener

Virginia Kylberg, gifted artist

Marek/Janci Design and Lucyna Green, whose cover and book designs brought the words to life

Patsy Loyd, Sales Manager for Fearon Teacher Aids

Sandy Hatch, Sherie Zander, and Ann Alper, marriage, family, and child counselors

Debbie Prestine, Joann Burch, Davida Kristy, and Betsy Jackson, teachers

Elaine Bradish, Vice President of Operations for SIDS (Sudden Infant Death Syndrome)

Laurie Prestine, Jimmy O'Connor, Kay Thompson, and Lisa McCreary, friends who experienced unexpected deaths in their families

Jeffrey Prestine, Communications Major

Nadine Davidson, Celeste Mannis, and Karen Eustis, fellow authors

Frances Singleton and Joanne Singleton, wise beyond their years

Herb Singleton, Scott Prestine, John Singleton, Geraldine Prestine, and Jim Kachidurian, loyal supporters

Contents

Preface

It is not a love of writing or money that brought me to the point of writing this material. It is my love of children. My goal in developing this program was to provide insight into the emotions children feel after the death of someone that they love.

I wrote *Helping Children Cope with Death* as a resource intended to help adults help young children through the feelings most children experience after the death of someone that they love. Often adults don't realize that children need guidance and support through their grief as well. Some adults feel children will simply outgrow sad feelings or, even worse, that children are too young to experience grief. Many adults don't know what to say, don't understand what the children are feeling, or don't feel qualified to help. This guide will hopefully provide the information necessary for adults to feel confident helping children help themselves through the grieving process.

About *Someone Special Died*

The *Someone Special Died* picturebook is designed to help children identify and deal with the various stages of mourning following the death of a loved one. Read the book and discuss the story with children as a prelude to using the activities outlined in this resource.

In the story, someone a young child loves very much has died. The little girl remembers the times she spent with her loved one—going for walks, skipping stones, and playing catch. She asks her mother what happens when someone dies. Her mother simply and gently explains that a body stops working and that nothing could have been done to keep her loved one alive. Everything dies, her mother explains.

The young girl feels angry and slams the door. She feels sad and nothing seems to make her happy. She doesn't want to play with her friends and prefers to just be alone. Finally, as the young girl accepts the death of her loved one, she begins to feel better. She decides to a make a scrapbook to hold her special memories. She finally accepts the fact that her loved one will never be coming back, but that she will always have her happy memories.

Introduction

Television bombards the average person with coverage of death for family viewing, including graphic details. Headlines in the newspaper detail violence, war, and death, and violence has become almost a nightly form of family entertainment, whether viewed at home or at a local movie theater. Even children's programs, like Saturday morning cartoons, feature characters who often meet violent ends.

With such intense exposure to death, it would seem that people, young and old, would be comfortable discussing the subject. Quite the contrary, discussion of death on a personal level is uncomfortable for many people, regardless of age. It is not unusual for people to avoid the word "death" when speaking of a person who has died. People tend to use euphemisms, such as "passed away," "passed on," or "left us." In 1965, psychiatrist Elisabeth Kübler-Ross, a foremost authority on death, began her ground-breaking studies at Billings Memorial Hospital in Chicago by interviewing terminally ill patients. At last, people talked about death and their feelings about it. Today there are books, articles, television shows, classes, and terminal illness and bereavement support groups.

Despite these breakthroughs, sharing feelings about death is still quite difficult for many people. In some ways, the feelings associated with death are more removed today than ever before. In the past, families took care of one another when someone was ill, and many people died at home surrounded by loved ones. Today, a majority of our elderly and sick live in convalescent homes and the ill usually die in hospitals.

Even though it is hard to express feelings about death, it is something that we all experience. *Helping Children Cope with Death* is a guide to help teachers, parents, and other adults assist children in understanding death and the feelings they might experience. This resource provides practical suggestions and activities for communicating with children, recognizing their emotional reactions, and helping them cope with their grief.

What to Say:
Communicating Clearly

According to psychiatrist Elisabeth Kübler-Ross, children at different stages of development have different perceptions of death. Toddlers may think that a person who has died will be coming back. They have a difficult time understanding death's finality. Three to five-year-olds mainly associate death with sleep and the absence of movement. And, children between the ages of five and nine often have a great fear of death. By age nine or ten, children usually view death as something that happens to everyone and understands its finality. Because of these mixed and varied perceptions, it is important to carefully word the message that you deliver to children concerning death.

When Should I Talk to a Child About Death?

It is better to approach the topic of death with children before they experience it firsthand through the loss of someone they love. Reading a picturebook, such as *Someone Special Died*, and openly discussing the story with children will better prepare them to cope with the emotions they will likely experience.

When someone dies that they love, children should be told the truth immediately. Whether it be the death of a pet, classmate, friend, neighbor, parent, or other family member, it is essential to communicate clearly in a loving and natural way. Listen to children, comfort them, and encourage them to talk. Time and understanding will help them work through their grief. After children have been given an initial explanation, continue discussion about the loss at ordinary, daily moments. For example, if a child looks distracted or sad and you believe it's due to the death of a person he or she loves, you might gently ask "Are you thinking about Grandma?"

What Should I Say?

Be open and honest with children. Communicate in words that children can understand based on their age and abilities. Explain that "dead" means that the person's body has stopped working and won't work anymore. The loved one's body will not do the things it used to, such as walk, talk, and hear. The person won't feel any of the feelings he or she used to feel, such as sadness, anger, or hurt.

It is important to tell most children the cause of death of the person that they care about. Discuss the fact that nothing lives forever. Bodies grow old and tired and finally stop working. Plants die, animals die, and people die, as is explained in the story. Use examples in nature to help children understand that death eventually occurs to all living things.

If the death involved illness, invite a doctor or nurse to speak to the class to help give a clear description of the circumstances associated with the death of the loved one. Discuss how doctors are always learning about new cures for illnesses.

It is often easier for children to relate to a new loss if they are reminded of some other loss they have experienced. Everybody has lost something in their lifetime. Remind children of less painful losses and separations they have experienced, such as going to school for the first time, losing a favorite toy, and so on. This will help children better understand their new feelings of loss, but be sure not to compare the losses.

In families where religion plays a central role, children can also be helped by the explanations and comfort offered by their faith. However, keep in mind that many children take statements literally. For example, one child was told God scooped up Uncle John and took him to heaven. The child became afraid to play in open spaces for fear God would come to scoop him up as well.

Help eliminate confusion and misconceptions some young children may have by avoiding euphemisms. Try not to use words like "passed away," "gone on," or "left us." If a child is told that Grandpa has gone on a very long journey for a very, very long time, he or she will get the message that someone he or she loves has left without even saying good-bye. This can make children feel angry and abandoned. If a child is told that someone has died after being sick, that child may develop fears that normal illnesses are fatal. Do not compare death to sleep—"Aunt Mary is in eternal sleep." This explanation may lead children to fear that when they go to sleep, they might never wake up again.

Don't try to cover up your own feelings with the idea that you are protecting children from the pain. Children may feel more stress when adults don't share their true feelings. Express your own emotions to children and encourage them to respond. It is important to let children know you are grieving, too. Often children model adult behaviors. If you keep your feelings to yourself, children may do the same. Encourage children to talk. Assure them that it is okay to say "I can't believe he is dead," "I'm so angry she died," "Sometimes I want to yell at everyone," "Sometimes I just want to cry and cry," or, "Sometimes I want to stay in bed all day."

After explaining the circumstances of the death of a loved one, explain to children that their feelings of anger, blame, or sadness are normal, and that it's okay to wish the person who has died would come back to life. Reassure children that one death doesn't mean that more are on the way.

How Will Children React?

All children react uniquely to a death of someone they are close to. Even children within the same family may experience varying reactions. Reactions may become apparent anywhere from a few days to a few months or even years later.

Children will undoubtedly have many questions. Answer their questions directly, briefly, and honestly. There are no easy or correct answers—it's okay for you to say "I don't know." Often it is difficult to know how much information to give children about death. Answer questions that children ask, not what you think they should be asking. Avoid lengthy answers overloaded with explanations beyond a child's comprehension. Think through your explanations so children don't become unnecessarily frightened or confused.

Remember, children don't usually ask questions beyond their level of emotional readiness. Encourage children to write down questions that they may feel uncomfortable asking aloud. Here are some examples of typical questions to expect.

"Why can't they fix Grandpa?"
"When will he come back?"
"Can she hear me?"
"Is she sleeping?"
"Does this mean someone else is going to die?"
"How old was he? How old are you?"
"Why did she die?"
"Why couldn't she get better?"
"Did I do it?"
"Who is going to take care of me now?"
"Will I die?"
"What is death?"
"What happens after death?"

No one person can answer all the questions children have — not Mom or Dad, friend, teacher, or therapist. Children assimilate information from various sources. On the basis of the information they receive, they formulate their own opinions. The activities in this resource guide will help children gain more information.

After a death, some children experience a change in attitude or behavior. Some reactions may include:

loud, aggressive behavior
excessively nice behavior
lack of motivation
indifference
defensive behavior
joking attitude
dependency
panic
exhaustion
hyperactivity
destructive behavior
regression

Children will also experience a variety of emotions that will take them through the stages of mourning identified in the next section. Listen to children and be in tune to their feelings. It is important for children to know you are really listening to them. A level of trust develops as children realize you do listen and you do care. Try to position yourself at their eye level. Sit on small chairs or on the floor. Standing gives a sense of urgency, as though you don't have time to listen. Being at children's eye level makes you their equal — an important element when dealing with this sensitive issue.

What to Expect: Recognizing Reactions

After conducting hundreds of interviews, Kübler-Ross found that people who are dying pass through five distinct emotional stages. She also noted that survivors who are grieving often pass through these same emotional stages. These are the reactions you can expect from children who have experienced the death of a loved one.

shock and denial
anger
bargaining
depression and withdrawal
acceptance

There is no definitive length of time that adults or children stay in any one of these five stages. A stage may last minutes or years and the order of the five stages may vary. It is also possible to slide back and forth from one emotional stage to another.

Each stage is clearly represented in the book *Someone Special Died*. A child expressing anger may become loud and argumentative. It is helpful for children to understand that their feelings may be erratic for a while. Knowing what to expect and assuring them that these erratic feelings are normal will help children cope in the long run. Here are some statements that are characteristic of each of the five stages of mourning.

Shock and Denial

"I don't think he died."

"She's sick. The doctor will make her better."

"He just needs to sleep."

"He'll go away for a while, then he'll get better and come back."

"I know she'll come back. She told me she'd always be with me."

"I know he's coming back. He said so."

"No matter what you say, you'll never change my mind."

Anger

"I'll never go to the doctor again. The doctor made my mom die."

" He didn't even say good-bye."

"I hate her for dying."

"I hate the doctor for killing him."

"I'll never love anyone that much again."

Bargaining

"It's my fault Mom died. If I hadn't . . . "

"Am going to die, too?"

"If only I had . . . , Grandpa would still be alive."

"I wish I were dead."

"You're supposed to be old when you die."

"Are you going to die?"

Depression and Withdrawal

"I'm so lonely."

"No one understands."

"Why did this happen to me?"

"I'm scared I'm going to die."

"I sleep with the light on because he died at night with the light off."

"He was my only friend."

"Why did she leave me? Why won't she come back?"

Acceptance

"I know I will never see her again."

"We can never go to the park together again, but I will always remember the days we did. We had such fun."

"Grandpa died, but I will always love him."

"I will miss her, but I know she still loves me."

Before you encourage children to speak up, it is important for you to know how you will react to their feelings. The topic of death sparks emotions within most people. Death tends to make you focus on yourself, your life, and your sense of being. It is important for you to work through your own thoughts and feelings before you can help children work through theirs.

It is not uncommon for children who have experienced a death to feel a barrage of miserable feelings. Not knowing how to cope with these feelings, some children fear these feelings will last forever. It is possible that some children become so accustomed to negative emotions that they feel guilty enjoying life. The sooner children understand their feelings, the sooner they begin to work through them. To help children identify and understand their emotions, try some of the following activities.

Emotion Triggers

Keep in mind that a random remark or something in a child's environment may trigger a child's sense of loss at any time. Some children may deny their feelings and seem to undergo no disruption in daily activities. Later, a seemingly insignificant event occurs that causes an extreme reaction. Try a picture-association activity to stimulate discussion and give children opportunities to express their feelings. Present a set of pictures cut from magazines or pictures children have drawn. Invite children to express how each picture makes them feel.

Mirror Messages

Help children learn to express their needs by imitating emotions in a mirror. As children make the expressions, talk about what their face is saying.

How Do You Feel Today?

It is important for an adult to help children identify their feelings without telling the child how he or she should be feeling. Present a set of face cards that display various emotions. Invite children to choose the faces that best portray how they are feeling. Encourage children to explain their choices.

Feeling Faces

Children trying to cope with the death of someone they love may react differently in an individual or group setting than they did before the death. Actions may become exaggerated. Children may become more quiet, withdrawn, sullen, depressed, angry, aggressive, babyish, or needy. Encourage children to draw various expressions (sad, mad, frustrated, lonely, jealous, scared) on paper plates. Make a hole through all of the plates and attach string or yarn to the plate collection. Children can flip the plates according to how they feel. Ask children to also describe how they feel using words as well.

Many Hats

Place a variety of hats (cowboy hat, helmet, fancy hats, and so on) in a pile on the floor or on a table. Invite children to try on different hats and look at themselves in a mirror. Encourage children to describe how the hats make them look and feel. Invite children to add facial expressions and body movements to go with each new look.

What to Do: How Activities Help

Activities are an excellent way of encouraging children to express their feelings. The practical activities in this resource guide help children understand their emotions. They reassure children that it is normal to have strong feelings and reactions after the death of a loved one. And, they give children specific tasks to help them work through their grief. The activities in this resource are not intended to be a cure for children who have severe emotional or adjustment problems related to the death of a loved one. These children may need to receive professional guidance.

Suggestions for Implementing the Activities

- Don't tell children how to feel or react. Like adults, children need to express their own feelings. Give basic directions, but allow children freedom to create their own projects with little outside interference. Their projects will be more meaningful to them if children create according to their own rules in a loosely structured environment.

- Provide a play environment around which activities can be introduced. This type of environment encourages children to approach feelings and thoughts that might otherwise be too uncomfortable to deal with.

- Some children choose to engage in one activity over and over and not to participate in any others. That's okay. An activity may be perfect for one child and not useful for another. Feel free to rotate activities depending on the needs of the children.

- The thoughts and feelings children experience while doing a project are the most important considerations. Feelings the children held for the loved one when the person was alive are often re-experienced. Tears may follow. Comment on children's sad feelings and then help them put their feelings into words.

- It may be difficult for you to accurately access how a child who is dealing with death is doing and what stage of mourning he or she is experiencing. If you have questions about the adjustment some children are making, then it is wise to save examples of their work. Share your findings with family members or a school or child therapist. Include a date on the back of each activity so chronological progression is easy to follow. You could also keep notes or comments on verbal responses to share with family members or a child's therapist.

The little girl in the story *Someone Special Died* made a scrapbook to hold all of the memories she shared with her loved one. This is a great way for children to work through their feelings and can be an ongoing activity. Encourage children to make scrapbooks of their favorite memories of their loved ones. This will give children lasting and concrete reminders to look through and help them remember important moments. Suggest that children include pictures (photographs or drawings) and words to recreate special and lasting memories. Encourage children to design front and back covers for their scrapbooks as well. The books can be bound using staples, three-ring binders, or even placed in magnetic photo albums. Be sure to include blank pages so children can add memories as time goes by. Children can add to the scrapbooks as they participate in other tasks in this resource, too. Invite children to keep all of their projects and completed activities in the scrapbooks.

Children who share the loss of a loved one can make a combined group scrapbook. For example, a group of neighborhood children may be close to a neighbor who has died. A class may share the loss of a classmate. Or, a class may share special memories of a classmate's parent who has recently died. Depending on the situation, children could pass this group scrapbook on to the family of the loved one who died or the scrapbook could be placed in the school library.

The activities that follow are divided into sections that relate to the five stages of mourning as depicted in the book *Someone Special Died*. After listening to children's comments and questions and helping them express how they are feeling, choose activities that are appropriate to meet their particular emotional needs.

Shock and Denial

"I miss him. I can't believe I won't ever see him again. Sometimes I pretend he's still alive."

These words from the book *Someone Special Died* convey the feelings children have when they are experiencing the shock and denial that often follow the death of a loved one.

Shock and denial occur almost immediately. During this stage, a first reaction might be "No, there must be a mistake. You're wrong. He's not dead." Some children may gloss over the death and pretend that nothing has happened. These children don't appear to have any out-of-the-ordinary feelings or reactions. These children's outward appearances convey the message that life goes on as usual. In some cases, the loved one's death is so painful that it is easier for these children to cope by staying in denial.

Some children pretend the person who has died is still alive. You may become aware of denial in a child if he or she does not use the word "death" or does not refer to the person as having died. Children may continue to talk to the person who has died or continue to associate certain toys or activities with that person. Sometimes children's dreams of the loved one may seem so real to them that they awaken convinced that the person's death did not actually happen. Children may even think they saw the person who has died.

The temporary numbness of shock and denial allows children to begin adjusting to the death before more severe feelings of loss begin to surface. The next stages may zigzag and the duration for each stage is entirely individual. Some children may even skip some of the stages.

Activities that give children opportunities to interact with the person who has died through their memories help children work through these feelings of shock and denial. These activities will help children move closer to accepting the death of their loved one as well.

Path of Life
Helping children understand the life cycle often helps them understand their reactions toward death. The cause of death is different from person to person, so it is important to discuss how and when in the life cycle the person died. Discuss how a life cycle includes stages, such as prenatal, infancy, childhood, teenager, young adult, middle age, older adult, and elderly. Help children design a wall mural on a large piece of paper using the stages of life to make a timeline. Using the timeline as a guide, discuss where in the life cycle the person was when he or she died. Explain that all people are born and eventually die. Gently explain to children that no one lives forever.

Take a Look Around

It is comforting to children to know how different people around them might react to death. Encourage children to look at others who are sharing their grief. Describe to children what they might be seeing. For example, "Uncle Peter might sit very quietly by himself. You might see Aunt Ida crying." Explain to children that it's okay to want to be alone, to cry, to talk about how they feel, or just be themselves.

Plant Flowers

Sometimes it is easier to talk about death with children as it relates to a plant rather than a human. Open conversation about the life span of a plant can help children gain an understanding of what they are experiencing. Help children plant flower seeds. Encourage children to care for the garden and watch the seeds grow into tiny sprouts, become mature plants, and blossom. Discuss how flowers also eventually die. Explain that even with good care, flowers won't live forever. Discuss with the children how they will feel when the flowers die. Invite children to save flower blossoms and allow them to dry. Help children press the dried flowers and keep them as memories in their scrapbooks.

Pet Experiences

Some children's first exposure to death is through the loss of a pet. If this is the case, consider the experience an opportunity to explain death. Do not shield children from the death experience. Children tend to be more willing to ask questions about a pet than a human. Discuss the varying lengths of life cycles of different pets, such as birds, frogs, fish, hamsters, cats, snakes, dogs, and ants. Gently remind children that nothing lives forever.

Make a List

Many times there are reminders in daily life that cause memories of the person who has died to surface. It is important for children to share these memories and not deny that they exist. Hanging onto the thoughts and feelings can be extremely lonely. Recommend that children make lists of words, names, phrases, book titles, TV shows, favorite songs, foods, and places that remind them of the person who has died. Reassure children that it's okay to enjoy the memories. Encourage children to allow the items on their lists to remind them of positive memories of the person they loved, rather than trigger their sense of loss.

Puppet Play

A puppet that in some way reminds children of the person who has died can be a tool to help release feelings and reactions. Help children make puppets using socks, hats, or other materials. Use clothing or other objects that belonged to the person who has died, if possible. Sew or glue on buttons for faces. Stuff the puppets with old rags and tie them closed. Encourage children to interact with the puppets and say things they would like to say to their loved one. Children may even find comfort in sleeping with their puppets.

Encourage Questions

Encourage children to ask questions or make comments about the death of a loved one. Talking about the death makes it seem more real and helps most children move out of shock and denial. Some children may want to write their thoughts in scrapbooks or journals.

Anger

**"He shouldn't have left me. I loved him.
It's not fair. Sometimes I feel so mad, I want
to yell, or hit my pillow, or slam the door."**

These words from the book *Someone Special Died* convey the feelings children have when they are experiencing anger as a result of the death of a loved one.

Many children feel tremendous anger when they feel the loss of a loved one. This is a normal response. The closer the survivor is to the person who has died, the more anger there may be. There are different types of anger. Children tend to feel angry because they feel deserted or abandoned by the person who has died. It doesn't feel right to be angry at the loved one, so many children also feel guilty about their anger. Another type of anger comes from a feeling that somehow they were responsible for the death. Children may think that they were too noisy, their rooms were too messy, or that they were bad. Because of their mistakes, they feel partly responsible for the death.

Their anger may express itself through unruly behavior in group situations, temper tantrums, yelling, or fighting. Family, friends, God, or the world in general may be targets of the children's fury.

Before reaching the stage of acceptance, children need to work through their anger and their guilt feelings. When children are able to release their anger and forgive the person who has died for leaving them, it is easier for children to move on with their lives. The following activities help children vent their anger in constructive and safe ways without encouraging aggressive behavior.

Healthy Expressions of Anger
Hitting other children or yelling and screaming are unacceptable expressions of anger. Give children who express such anger pillows or punching bags. Encourage children to vent their angry feelings by taking out their aggressions on the pillows or punching bags instead.

Exercise
For many children, exercise can reduce emotional stress. Encourage children who have a lot of undirected energy or pent-up hostility to run laps outside or engage in other physical activities that will prevent them from using their energy in disruptive ways. Make sure children understand that this physical activity is not a punishment for being angry. Invite children to play non-competitive games, ride bicycles, play ball, or do gymnastics.

Music and Movement
Music and body movement can be very effective tools for individual and group expression. Choose appropriate music

and invite children to use body movements to express their moods. Select music that gives children opportunities to express their anger and also music that creates a sense of peace and serenity.

Create with Clay

Some children may have difficulty expressing their feelings verbally. Invite such children to use a hands-on approach to release their emotions. Give children lumps of clay and encourage them to create. Invite children to say anything they want to the clay and feel free to punch it, poke it, pat it, and pound it.

Write a Poem

Encourage older children to write about their anger at feeling abandoned. Help children express any feelings of guilt about causing the death of the person that they loved. Encourage younger children to dictate their thoughts as you record them. Help children understand that they had no control over or responsibility for the death of the person who has died. Invite children to decorate the borders of their papers. Send the papers to the family of the person who has died or put the children's writings in a scrapbook. Respect the fact that some children may not want to share their writings.

Relax and Rest

Occasionally, because of stress, children may have trouble sleeping. Relaxation techniques may help some children. When the room is dark and quiet, suggest that children lie flat on their backs with their arms and legs extended. Direct children to close their eyes and count backwards beginning at 10. Starting with the toes and working upward, encourage children to visualize each part of their body relaxing and falling asleep. Remind children to breathe deeply.

Imaginary Trip

An effective way to help children relax is to guide them through a peaceful imaginary trip using visualization.

Suggest that children visualize the following scene as you describe it.

"You are walking on the beach. Feel the warm sun enveloping your body. Listen to the sound of the soothing ocean waves. Feel the soft sand under your feet. Hear the sound of the birds as they quietly float through the air above your head. Feel the gentle breeze on your back. Now pretend you are floating off the ground and into the clouds as a gentle breeze blows through your hair. Imagine the soft, fluffy clouds brushing against your cheeks. Sail through the sky over your house. Gently come down, down, down and land safely in your bed. Snuggle into your cozy bed and sleep, sleep, sleep."

Gather Photographs

When children share the experience of the death of a mutual friend or acquaintance, encourage them to gather photographs of their shared experiences. Not all children will have access to photographs. Invite these children to draw pictures about their relationship with the person who has died. Photographs and pictures can help children relive the relationship and remember important moments. Glue the photographs and pictures to construction paper. Draw a frame or border around each one. Place the photographs and pictures in a scrapbook.

Quiet Chat

Encourage children to express their feelings of anger to the loved one that has died by directing their comments to pictures of the person. Sit down in a quiet place with grieving children and encourage them to talk to the picture and express all of their positive and negative feelings. This is often a helpful technique for saying good-bye.

Encourage Questions

Encourage children to talk about their anger and guilt so they understand what is going on inside them. Many times bottled-up feelings explode if there is no avenue for expression.

Bargaining

**"If I had been there, I wouldn't have let
him die. But Mom says I couldn't have done anything to
help keep him alive. Mom says everything dies."**

These words from the book *Someone Special Died* convey
the feelings children have when they are experiencing the
stage of bargaining as a result of the death of a loved one.

It is common for some children to feel responsible in some
way for the death of the person that they care about. Guilt
feelings may stay with many children, especially if, during
an angry period when the individual was alive, they had
hateful or unkind thoughts toward the loved one. Or, sometimes children may have wished the person dead. In these
cases, guilt feelings are almost a certainty. Reassure children

that their thoughts are normal. Also reassure them that thoughts can't make someone die. Explain that it is not possible to wish someone dead and thereby cause the death to happen.

Once in a while children may think they have not been good companions. A child may think "If only I had visited more, if only I had said how much I loved her, if only I had been more quiet, or if only I had been there, I could have helped keep him alive." Some children do not possess the reasoning capabilities to distinguish between thoughts and deeds.

These guilty feelings may be so intense that a child feels guilty for surviving and wishes he or she would die as well. The guilt may be so deep that children are unaware of its presence. Reassure children that they are not responsible for the person's death.

The following activities will help children recognize and work through their feelings of guilt or regret.

Talk About Guilt

Encourage children to talk about their feelings instead of holding them inside. Use the following sentences as conversation starters.

"If you could see the person once more, what three things would you say?"
"If you could see the person once more, what three things would you want the person to say to you?"
"If you could see the person once more, what three things would you do?"

Puppet Talk

It is often easier for children to express their feelings through puppets, rather than speaking for themselves. Provide puppets at a play center. Encourage children to create dialogues with one another using the puppets. Listen for insights into children's feelings and emotions as you observe the puppet play.

A Picture Worth a Thousand Words

Children often experience a variety of unsettling feelings and emotions after the death of a relative or friend. These feelings may result in a number of reactions. It is often difficult for many children to translate their emotions into words or express their feelings. It may be easier for some children to express their feelings by drawing. Invite children to draw pictures to represent how they are feeling. Encourage children to draw whatever comes to mind and to use whatever colors they would like. After the pictures are complete, encourage children to talk about them and explain what the drawings show.

Write a Poem

Encourage older children to write about their feelings of guilt or regret in a poem. Help children express any feelings of guilt about causing the death of the person that they cared about. Encourage younger children to dictate their thoughts as you record them. Help children understand that they had no control over or responsibility for the death of their loved one.

Make a Gift

Some children's feelings of guilt or regret can be eased by giving children the opportunity to make gifts for the family of the person who has died. Children may also find comfort in making something for themselves that they feel the person would have wanted them to have. Children can keep the gifts, or give the gifts to the family of the person who has died. If children choose to give the gifts away, suggest they draw pictures of the gifts to include in a scrapbook.

Make a Book

Some children are prolific writers and others love to draw. Encourage children to write or illustrate picturebooks about their relationship with the loved one who has died. For those children who find writing difficult, encourage them to draw pictures about their relationship instead. Create brightly colored covers from construction paper. Staple the writings or pictures together to make books.

Trouble Box

Invite children to imagine a big box that can hold all of their troubles and worries. Encourage children to mentally place each feeling of guilt or regret, one by one, into the imaginary box. When the box is full and their minds are clear, have children imagine putting the box away.

Fantasy Play

When very young children are grieving, they know they feel bad, but often do not have the vocabulary to explain what is going on inside of them. Give children an opportunity to use body language and gestures to convey their feelings. Set up a dramatic-play center and encourage children to act out their feelings through play and imagination.

Encourage Questions

Guilt is a heavy burden for children to carry. Encourage them to express their feelings. Remind children that no thought is too terrible for them to share.

Depression and Withdrawal

"Sometimes I feel so sad, that nothing makes me happy. I just want to cry and cry. Sometimes I don't want to play with anyone . . . . I just want to be alone."

These words from the book *Someone Special Died* convey the feelings children have when they are experiencing depression or withdrawal as a result of the death of a loved one.

Depending on how close children were to the person who has died, the emptiness they feel may lead to an overwhelming sense of loss. Children mourn for the loved one, but they also mourn for the loss in their own lives. Reactions can range from overly weepy to almost completely withdrawn.

Both reactions could be indications of depression. Loneliness, fear, and abandonment are also feelings that may signal depression in a child.

What may seem like an overreaction may actually indicate strong feelings of sadness. A child may cry for what seems like a long time. If you feel it is appropriate, put your arm around a child who feels like crying. Give children crying time. It is not possible for someone else to take away children's grief, but patience and understanding can provide some comfort.

Some children appear to be quiet and withdrawn, but don't cry or allow their emotions to surface outwardly. These children often appear stable. Adults tend to be more comfortable with children who show little emotion, so sometimes these children don't receive the emotional support they actually need. Children who keep their feelings inside tend to take longer to do their healing.

It is important for children to discuss their grief so they don't learn to bury their feelings. If children consistently bury their feelings, it may be difficult for them as they get older to develop close relationships. There is no magic formula to make grief disappear. Listen and support children to help them work through their sorrow.

The following activities will help children express their sadness. With these activities, children can feel comfortable and not think adults are trying to pry into their thoughts.

Tape Recording
Some children feel more comfortable expressing their feelings when their thoughts do not seem so public. Provide children with an area where they feel a sense of privacy. Give children a stuffed animal and an easy-to-use tape recorder. Show children how to record and how to listen to their taped conversations. Encourage children to say anything they want into the tape recorder. Suggest that children speak to the stuffed animals, if that makes them feel more

comfortable. Later, with permission from the children, listen to the tape recordings together. Invite children to comment on the recordings and discuss their feelings.

Remember When?

Depressed or withdrawn children often suppress their feelings and avoid remembering what life was like when the loved one was alive. Use prompts to encourage children to express their thoughts, such as "Remember when Grandma took you to the lake? Remember how much she loved you?" and so on.

What Makes You Happy?

Some children forget the faults of the person who has died. They remember the person as perfect and therefore no one else can make them happy. Invite children to brainstorm lists of things that make them happy. By making these lists, children will become more aware of ways they can begin to feel happy again, in spite of their loss.

Paper-Bag Puppets

Many times children are more comfortable sharing their feelings when they have someone or something to hide behind. A puppet can be the perfect tool to provide children with this feeling of safety and comfort. Encourage children to create a puppet show. To make the puppets, help children cut facial features out of colored construction paper and glue them to brown lunch bags. The grieving child's puppet can play the role of the character who experienced the death of a loved one or play the role of the person who has died. Encourage children to act out their feelings of anger, fear, loneliness, or sadness.

Support System

It is important for children who are dealing with death to have someone they can talk to. Both children and adults need encouragement and support. Encourage children to give some thought to the people they feel most comfortable talking to. Urge children to make an effort to share some of their feelings with these people.

Write a Letter

Writing a letter may help some withdrawn children express their feelings. Guide children to write (or dictate) how much they miss and love the person who has died. Encourage children to add their own special thoughts and feelings.
Children can place the letters in envelopes and actually mail the letters to the family of the person who has died. Or, children can keep the letters in a scrapbook.

Healthy and Happy

Children may often display physical signs of their emotional conditions. Depressed or withdrawn children may seem to lack energy or stamina. During stressful periods, it is wise for children to eat balanced meals in order to keep their energy level as even as possible. Discuss healthy foods with children and provide foods in any meals served that include protein, complex carbohydrates, fruits, and vegetables.
Invite children to draw pictures or cut them from magazines to make posters of healthy foods.

Physical Signs

When children withhold their emotional feelings, these feelings often surface in the form of physical disorders. Children may exhibit restlessness, complain of aches and pains, lack an appetite, or have difficulty sleeping during times of emotional stress. Be aware of the physical conditions of children and be prepared to discuss, if necessary, their needs.

Encourage Questions

Drawing out children's depressed feelings helps them become aware of their own emotions. Understanding their feelings helps them gain control. Encourage children to talk about their emotions. Questions and discussion can help relieve children's depression.

Acceptance

**"... when I think about the fun we had together,
I feel better. I want to make a scrapbook,
so I'll always remember our good times ....
He died and I know he won't be coming back.
But with my scrapbook, I'll never forget him."**

These words from the story *Someone Special Died* convey the feelings children have when they finally reach the stage of acceptance of the death of one they love.

The death of someone they love is quite traumatic to a child. When someone they love dies, it is wise to include most children in the mourning process, rather than exclude them. Sometimes adults feel they are protecting children by not exposing them to funerals, memorial services, and so on. Excluding children may lengthen the time it takes for them to accept the loss. Usually, when children are included in the mourning process, it helps children begin their emotional progression to acceptance. Allowing children to attend funerals gives them the opportunity to say good-bye, which is a necessary form of closure.

If children attend wakes or funerals, it is important for them to know what to expect. Crying is an appropriate behavior at a funeral, but children need to know before the service if there will be much crying. Seeing adults cry may make some children uncomfortable, yet give other children permission to release their own sadness. Keep in mind that various cultures, and even families within the same culture, share different traditions.

In some cultures, extended families include parents, children, grandparents, cousins, aunts, or uncles who live together under one roof. An extended family can be as close as a primary family unit, which includes only parents and children. The death of a cousin in an extended family may be a severe loss to another cousin. Cultural traditions may include:

Sitting with the person who has died.
Viewing an open casket.
Kissing or touching the loved one who has died.
Attending a wake.
Attending a funeral service in a church, temple, home, or mortuary.
Attending a graveside service.
Crying or wailing at the service.
Using pallbearers.
Attending a cremation.
Attending a family gathering after the service.
A mourning period where family members wear black, do not listen to music, cook, work, or play.
Adult family members who openly show their feelings and cry over a long period of time.
Adult family members who show little or no emotion.

It is impossible to know the feelings of children or how long it will take them to accept the death of someone that they love. Some children may accept a death more readily than an adult or may need a longer period of adjustment. The progression of feelings depends on the individual, whether an adult or a child. A few children will need special help working through the stages of mourning.

Help children understand that acceptance of the death of a loved one doesn't mean the person is forgotten. Help children create lasting memories of the person that they loved.

Act It Out

Acting out a children's picturebook or play can help some children feel a sense of closure. Picturebooks, because of their length, make good scripts for younger children. Using the story from *Someone Special Died* as a base, ask for additional story ideas or changes and write a script for the children. In the margins of the script, write the name of the child who will play each character. If children are old enough to read, make a copy for each one. Use a hi-liter marker to indicate individual character parts. Discuss the script with children to make sure they understand their parts. Encourage children to ad-lib and speak their feelings of denial, anger, sadness, or guilt and then finally, say good-bye. Elaborate props and costumes are unnecessary. Urge the actors to stray from the script to speak and act freely with little outside intervention.

A Special Token

Sometimes it can be helpful for children to keep something that reminds them of the one they loved. If possible, help children find a special token that they can keep as a constant reminder of the love they shared with the person who has died.

Good-Bye Gift

An effective way to help children realize the finality of death is to encourage them to make a good-bye gift for the loved one who has died. Invite children to think of special gifts, such as bouquets of flowers, drawings, poems, songs, or letters. Help children make their special gifts in honor of the one they loved.

In Memory Of . . .

Books can be donated to a library in memory of the person who has died. Particularly effective in a school setting where classmates have experienced the death of a peer, achievement awards, funds, scholarships, or a book purchase for the library can be established in that person's honor.

A Special Day

Special days are celebrated to remember people from history who have died, such as famous heroes, presidents, or those who have contributed in some way to the world. Invite children to select a special day to remember and honor someone they love—either individually or as a group. Children can celebrate the birth date of the person who has died or choose another day to remember the life of their loved one.

Saying Good-Bye

If children do not attend the funeral of a loved one who has died, it may be difficult for them to find the appropriate time or place to say good-bye. If possible, with permission from parents or guardians, take children to the cemetery where they can ask questions, express their feelings, or simply say good-bye. Invite parents or guardians to accompany you and the children. If a group of children share a common loss of a loved one, you could plan a memorial service for them to participate in, if they choose. Support the children as they think of words they would like to say at the service. Urge each child to say two or three specific things about the person who has died. Encourage children to remember what they did together. Urge them to express their feelings of denial, anger, sadness, fear, loneliness, regret, or guilt and then finally, say good-bye. Respect the wishes of those children who choose not to participate.

Plant a Tree

Plant a memorial tree in honor of the person who has died. Invite children to participate in the ceremony and help care for the tree as it grows. Point out how the tree will experience a cycle of life, just as people do. It will have a beginning and an end.

Outreach

Once their family and school environment feel safe, children may want to help others who are grieving. By helping other family members, friends, or neighbors over a death, children also benefit. Helping others gives most children a sense of control over their feelings and may lead to their acceptance of the death of the person that they cared about. Recommend that children visit a relative, friend, or neighbor of the person who has died. Suggest they discuss what they have in common with the person who has died, activities they did together, and how they feel about the death. Or, invite children to make a telephone call to a relative, friend, or neighbor. A phone call is usually uplifting to both the caller and the receiver. Children could also write a note and send a colorful picture to someone else who shares their grief. Explain to children that it is okay to talk openly about the person who has died.

Create a Gift

Suggest that children make special gifts in honor of the person who has died. These special gifts can be given to a friend, family member, or neighbor of the person who has died. By reaching out to comfort someone else who shares the same grief, children can accept their own feelings about the death of a loved one. Encourage children to use their creativity and imagination to make appropriate gifts. Suggestions might include decorating a card, making a collage, or painting a piece of tile.

Reach Out to a Peer

Many children don't know what to say to a friend after the friend has experienced the death of a loved one. It is not that friends don't care, they just don't know how to respond.

Help children reach out to a peer who has lost someone they love. If a child in the neighborhood or class has suffered the death of a loved one, invite the other children to support the child by composing a memory book. Propose that each child in the group design a colorful picture. Bind the pictures to form a book. Encourage the children to design a colorful cover. Then invite the children to give the memory book to the grieving child as a show of support.

Encourage Questions

Children may continue to have questions or comments about death for a long period of time. Weeks, months, and even years may go by before all the questions and feelings are uncovered. Encourage children to ask questions and talk about the death of their loved one, even though it may be several weeks since the person died.

Building Self-Esteem and Stability

Experiencing the death of a loved one can greatly affect a child's self-esteem. If children's self-esteem declines, so may their confidence in their actions. Doing both familiar and unfamiliar things may become difficult, which results in further lowered self-confidence. Children may have difficulty making simple decisions—deciding whether to read a book or play with a puzzle may seem bewildering to a child experiencing grief.

Children's sense of security can become unsteady because they may worry about who is going to die next. Some children are afraid they will lose another loved one or may worry that they themselves might die. Children need experiences that make them feel secure and loved and need reassurance both in words and actions. Stay with children, hug them frequently, and talk to them about upcoming plans. Try to keep as many things constant in their lives as possible. It is not a good idea to move away at this time or to alter normal daily routines, if at all possible.

Because young children lack sufficient language skills to express their needs, it is important to try to anticipate them. Make a conscious effort to give children hands-on attention, affection, and consistent reassurance. Use the following activities to increase children's self-esteem and help rebuild a secure and stable environment.

Decision-Making

The ability to make a decision gives children a sense of power over their lives and instills self-confidence. Offer two or three simple choices to children. For example, invite children to choose between two books or two puzzles. Ask children whether they want to play inside or outside. Invite children to decide how to rearrange a game cupboard. As children's confidence builds, offer more complex choices that require more thought.

Attention Givers

Some children vie for adult or peer attention at home or in a group by becoming unruly. Refusal to speak individually or in front of a group may be another bid for attention. Some children become excessively good or nice. Be aware that children who are experiencing loss need extra attention. Make a point to give grieving children special assignments, extra hugs, or words of encouragement.

Notes About Me

In order to rebuild self-esteem, some children need constant reminders of how special they are. Invite children to decorate shoeboxes. Whenever you notice children handling a task well, cooperating, helping, and so on, take the opportunity to let them know. Write your positive comments on small slips of paper and put them in children's decorated shoeboxes. It won't be long before the shoeboxes are full. Pick a special time to sit with each child and read through their accomplishments together.

What I Like About Me

It is usually easier for children who are depressed or withdrawn to talk about what is wrong with themselves rather than their good qualities. Encourage children to concentrate on what they like about themselves. Using a stop watch, give children one minute to name as many of their good qualities as they can think of.

I Know I Can

It is essential that children recognize their strengths and talents to develop higher self-esteem. Invite children to complete the following sentences.

"I know I can . . ."
"I am proud that I . . ."
"People like it when I . . ."
"A good idea I had was . . ."
"I like it when I . . ."
"I figured out how to . . ."

High-Flying Flags

Invite children to make flags that represent their unique qualities. Encourage children to include some of their favorite colors, foods, words, sounds, and special interests. Invite children to talk about their flags. Attach the flags to small wooden dowels. Encourage children to wave the flags in a high-flying parade.

A Book About Me

Encourage children to write a book about themselves. Younger children can make picturebooks. Invite children to read or tell about their books to friends or family members.

Friends

Friendship is extremely important for children who have suffered the loss of a loved one. Encourage children to focus on their friendships and find comfort in the fact that they are not alone. Invite children to finish the following sentences.

"I feel good when my friends . . ."
"I like my friends to . . ."

"My friends help me by . . ."
"I am a good friend because . . ."
"I know my friends will always . . . "

Compliment Connection

Some grieving children with low self-esteem have trouble accepting compliments. Provide children with opportunities to give and receive compliments. Help children understand that it's okay to feel good about themselves, even after losing someone they love. Make it a habit to point out the positive qualities you see in children.

Laugh and Love

Some children try to withdraw from life after the death of a loved one. Feelings ranging from guilt, fear, loneliness, pain, grief, and sadness interfere with children having fun, laughing, and just plain living. Give children opportunities to laugh by reading enjoyable books, browsing through the comic section of the newspaper, playing a game, or telling jokes. Explain to children that it's okay to laugh and enjoy themselves, even though a person they loved has died.

I'm Proud of Me

Invite children to close their eyes and relax. Encourage them to think back to a time when they did something they were very proud of. It may have been the first time they read a book, rode a bicycle, or won a race. Ask children to talk about their positive experiences.

Additional Resources

Berstein, Joanne E. Books to Help Children Cope with Separation and Loss. New York: R.R. Bowker Company, 1983.

This is an excellent bibliographic guide to both fiction and nonfiction books for young people, ages 3-16, on the themes of separation and loss. It is designed to provide information to adults in order for them to choose suitable books to serve the needs of grieving children.

Fassler, Joan. Helping Children Cope. New York: Macmillan, 1978.

This resource includes suggestions on how contemporary children's literature can help children grow, reduce their fears, and initiate open and honest communication. An entire section is devoted to ideas related to helping children deal with the stress associated with death.

Heegaard, Marge Eaton. Coping with Death & Grief. Minneapolis: Lerner Publications, 1990.

Young people's experiences with death are shared, as well as basic facts about death and suggestions for letting out feelings of sadness and anger.

Jackson, Edgar N. Telling a Child About Death. New York: Channel Press, 1965.

This book discusses the importance of honestly answering a child's questions about death.

Krementz, Jill. How It Feels When a Parent Dies. New York: Knopf, 1981.

Eighteen children from ages seven to sixteen speak openly and honestly about their experiences and feelings when a parent dies. Their stories give other children the sense that they are not alone and that certain feelings of guilt, confusion, and anger are normal.

Kübler-Ross, Elisabeth. On Children and Death. New York: Macmillan, 1983.

This resource provides both the children's viewpoint and the psychological aspects of death. It also deals with the psychology of terminally ill children and parent and child attitudes toward death.

LeShan, Eda. Learning to Say Goodbye: When a Parent Dies. New York: Macmillan, 1976.

In simple, direct language, the author discusses the questions, fears, and fantasies children have about the parent who has died and the people who are still alive. This resource reinforces the stages of mourning that we go through in the grieving process.

Lightner, Candy and Nancy Hathaway. Giving Sorrow Words. New York: Warner Books, 1990.

This book is the result of over 100 interviews with people whose lives were forever changed by the death of someone they loved. A special chapter is devoted to helping children who are grieving.

Morgan, John D. Young People and Death. Philadelphia: Charles Press, 1991.

Unlike other books on the subject of children and death that focus on concepts and theories, this book is concerned with the practical side of helping children and their families cope with death and loss. Today, children are threatened by the harsh reality of war, urban and domestic violence, murder, suicide, drug abuse, AIDS, and other tragedies inherent to the turbulent times in which we live.

Moriarty, David M. The Loss of Loved Ones. St. Louis: W.H. Green, 1983.

This resource includes the effects of a death in the family on personality development. It also deals with bereavement in children and parental deprivation.

Rando, Therese A. How to Go on Living When Someone You Love Dies. New York: Bantam, 1988.

This is a self-help book to provide the griever with the information necessary to better cope with a painful situation. Suggestions are given for helping children cope with death and mourning as well.

Richter, Elizabeth. Losing Someone You Love. New York: G.P. Putnam's Sons, 1986.

In this book, fifteen young people who have experienced the death of a brother or sister talk openly about their feelings. The children talk about their difficulties at home and school, as well as how they are learning to come to terms with their grief.

Rofes, Eric E. The Kids' Book About Death and Dying. Boston: Little Brown, 1985.

A group of students, ranging in ages from eleven to fourteen, explored the subject of death and dying under the direction of a teacher at Fayerweather Street School in Cambridge, Massachusetts. This book, written by and for kids, offers facts and advice to give young readers a better understanding of death.

Rudolph, Marguerita. *Should the Children Know? New York: Schocken Books, 1978.*

Gathering materials from her work with children and parents, the author explains how the very young can and should be taught about death — at school and home.

Schaefer, Dan and Christine Lyons. *How Do We Tell the Children? New York: Newmarket Press, 1986.*

This parents' guide provides the straightforward, uncomplicated language that will explain the facts of death to children and help them cope with their feelings of grief, fear, and loss.

Schiff, Harriet Sarnoff. *Living Through Mourning. New York: Viking, 1986.*

The author writes about emotions common to many survivors and discusses the process of grieving. A special chapter is devoted to dealing with bereavement in children.

Tatelbaum, Judy. *The Courage to Grieve. New York: Lippincott & Crowell, 1980.*

This self-help book provides the reader with specific help to recover and grow from grief. Some excellent advice is included for understanding the special grief of children.

Viorst, Judith. *"How Do You Talk to a Child About Death?" Redbook (May 1989): 32-34.*

This well-written article gives some practical suggestions for dealing with the array of emotions grieving children may experience. Whether the death be a pet, a grandparent, a sibling, or a friend, this article offers wise advice on how to talk to children about this sensitive subject.

Books for Children

Good children's books are excellent for stimulating conversation about sensitive issues, such as death. Children, regardless of age, will usually respond by listening, thinking, imagining, and then expressing their thoughts. Reading a book about a similar experience that a child is facing can help him or her vicariously work through and solve his or her own problems. Reading helps children realize they are not alone.

The following is an annotated bibliography of some quality literature selections dealing with death that are appropriate for preschool to third-grade children. Choose the books that best suit the needs of the children in your care.

About Dying
by Sara Bonnett Stein
New York: Walker and Company, 1974

This information-type book includes separate text for children and adults on each page. The adult text gives some insights into children's reactions to death. The children's text presents a realistic view of death based on two circumstances—the death of a bird and the death of a grandfather. Sharing this book can promote some valuable opportunities to discuss feelings, fears, and misconceptions about death and provide a forum for asking and answering questions.

The Accident
by Carol Carrick
New York: Clarion, 1976

This story vividly portrays a child's grief over the death of a dog killed by a truck. Christopher is furious at the driver, even though it is not the driver's fault. The young boy feels remorse for having taken the dog out that evening and he yells angry words. Eventually, Christopher talks with his father about the dog and cries freely. He then chooses a stone to place at the dog's grave as a way of saying good-bye. This is a moving and gentle story about loss.

Allison's Grandfather

by Linda Peavy

New York: Charles Scribner's Sons, 1981

Erica knows Allison's grandfather is dying. She has many questions, such as whether dying is going to be easy or hard, but she doesn't feel like talking about it—not just yet. This gentle story illustrates children's inner thoughts about death and the confusion they can experience. Instead of asking questions, Erica begins thinking of the fun and memorable experiences she shared with Allison's grandfather. She recalls adventurous stories Allison's grandfather told, such as the time he came head to head with a mother bear and her two cubs while gathering gooseberries. Throughout the story, questions continue to pop into Erica's head about death, but she still doesn't want to talk about them. She keeps many of her thoughts to herself. Finally, Mama answers the question Erica had not yet asked and tells her that Allison's grandfather has died that morning. Erica just wants to be held closely and rocked in her mother's lap.

Annie and the Old One

by Miska Miles

Boston: Little, Brown, 1971

In this story, a young Navajo girl has a special relationship with her grandmother. One day, the grandmother announces that she expects to die when the rug on the loom is finished. Annie refuses to believe that her grandmother will die and is determined to prevent it by making sure the rug is never completed. The grandmother at last convinces Annie that change and the cycle of life is inevitable. This story is excellent for helping children understand that death is a natural part of life. Another aspect to the story is that Annie's mother is at times reluctant to talk about the death of Annie's grandmother. This helps children be aware of other's reactions to death as well. The story also helps children understand that although they should feel free to share their thoughts and emotions, adults will not always feel comfortable doing so.

The Dead Bird
by Margaret Wise Brown
Reading, Massachusetts: Addison-Wesley, 1965

In this sensitive story, several children find a dead bird. The children notice that the bird is cold, has no heartbeat, and will never fly again, so they decide to bury it in the woods. While this section of the story may trigger discussion about the permanency of death, young children often wonder when a person or pet who has died will be coming back to life. The children in the story carefully plan a funeral for the dead bird. They wrap the bird in leaves, sing a special song, and make a grave marker. Every day, the children visit the burial site and put fresh flowers on the little bird's grave. By the end of the story, the children are busy playing and have since forgotten about visiting the dead bird's grave. This suggests that the children have accepted the little bird's death and are ready to move on to other things in their lives. This story may help children mourn by introducing them to the significance of a funeral or memorial service and how it commemorates the life of a loved one or pet.

Everett Anderson's Good-bye
by Lucille Clifton
New York: Holt, Rinehart and Winston, 1983

This beautiful book illustrates the stages of grief a young boy experiences after the death of his father. Each stage (shock and denial, anger, bargaining, depression and withdrawal, and acceptance) is identified by a vivid and specific description of Everett's feelings. These practical descriptions can be helpful in learning to recognize these stages in other children. Children often think that they will always feel the way they do at any given moment. This story provides an opportunity to encourage children to compare their feelings with Everett's and help children recognize that Everett's feelings changed over time, as theirs will, too. The story ends by pointing out Everett's acceptance of his father's death and the realization that although life has an end, love never stops.

The Fall of Freddie the Leaf
by Leo Buscaglia
Thorofare, New Jersey: Charles B. Slack, 1982

In this story, Freddie begins as a strong, firm leaf growing next to his best friend, Daniel. Daniel is the largest leaf on the limb and is the one who explains life to Freddie. He tells Freddie that they are part of a tree in a public park, that the tree has strong roots, and that the birds come to sit on their branch and sing morning songs. As each season passes, Daniel explains the changes to Freddie. The story helps children see that there are cycles in nature for all living things. As fall arrives, Daniel explains that all the leaves will change to beautiful colors and eventually die and fall from the tree. Freddie initially refuses to accept his fate and expresses his fears of the unknown. Through his determination to hang on, Freddie becomes the last leaf on the tree. Finally, as Freddie falls gracefully from the tree, he realizes that it doesn't hurt at all and he lands quite comfortably on the snowy ground below. The story ends by pointing out that Freddie's fall will contribute to another cycle in nature and, although it seems like the end, it is really only the beginning of other things to come.

Grandpa's Slide Show
by Deborah Gould
New York: Lothrop, Lee & Shepard, 1987

Sam and his little brother, Douglas, regularly sleep over at their grandparents' house. Grandpa always lets Sam work the control device, while they all watch slide shows and snuggle on the couch. Sam loves the click-click of each slide dropping in the projector and the family pictures shining brightly on the wall. But most of all, he loves his Grandpa. When Grandpa dies, the boys must deal with the loss. The warm, gentle pictures in this story convey a sense of family love and the strength that can be drawn from this love in times of grief. This book helps children who are mourning the loss of a loved one realize that family and friends can be a great comfort.

I'll Always Love You
by Hans Wilhelm
New York: Crown, 1985

This story conveys the sense of love and caring that a young boy and his dog share. Elfie and the young boy grow up together, but, since a dog's life is much shorter than a boy's, Elfie grows old and dies while the boy is still young. Each night, the young boy tells his dog that he will always love her. Even in death, he knows that this love will continue for all time. The child realizes that his dog will not return, yet refuses the offer for a new pet because he is not yet ready to love another. In the story, the young boy is given the opportunity to mourn his lost pet. The story shows it is important to allow children to mourn and not force them to put on a happy face or go on with life as usual when they've suffered a loss. The young boy takes comfort in the memory of the relationship he had with his dog and realizes that in time he will be ready for a new pet. And in time he will be able to love a new pet as much as he loved Elfie.

Lifetimes: The Beautiful Way to Explain Death to Children
by Bryan Mellonie and Robert Ingpen
New York: Bantam, 1983

Various life spans are explored in this book that gently makes the point that there is a beginning and an ending for everything alive. The book explains how all living things are born and all living things eventually die. How long something lives depends on what it is and what happens during its lifetime. The book describes the special lifetimes of plants, birds, fish, trees, animals, and even the tiniest insects. The connection is then made that people have lifetimes, too. And, just like other living things, there comes a time when they must die as well. Through this natural progression, children will understand that all lifetimes have beginnings and endings — an important concept for children to understand. This quietly beautiful book will help contribute to the acceptance of the death of a loved one.

My Grandson Lew
by Charlotte Zolotow
New York: Harper & Row, 1974

This story points out the importance of talking about feelings and openly communicating them to others. The story begins with Lew telling his mother how much he misses Grandpa. Lew's mother is surprised that Lew even remembers Grandpa, since he was so young when Lew and Grandpa knew each other. This is a gentle reminder not to underestimate the memory of and emotional involvement with a loved one that very young children may have. Lew then begins to describe the memories of Grandpa to his mother. He remembers Grandpa's scratchy beard, eye-hugs, strong arms, and the smell of Grandpa's pipe. Lew also tells his mother that he has been patiently waiting for Grandpa to return for a visit. Lew's mother finally explains that Grandpa has died. She never thought it was necessary to explain his death before because she didn't realize that Lew had missed his Grandpa. Lew's mother shares some of her memories of Grandpa, too, and together they feel less lonely and sad.

Nana Upstairs & Nana Downstairs
by Tomie de Paola
New York: G.P. Putnam's Sons, 1973

This is a gentle, easy book to explain death to the very young. It is the story of a young boy's relationship with his grandmother and great-grandmother. Because his great-grandmother always seemed to be in bed upstairs when he visited, he named her Nana Upstairs. Nana Upstairs would always tell Tommy that he could open the sewing box on the dresser and get some candy mints. In this story, Tommy realizes that when his great-grandmother dies, she will never be with him again. He knows that death is final and although he expresses his grief, he accepts the reality of great-grandmother's absence. Tommy's mother reassures him that Nana Upstairs will come back in memory whenever Tommy thinks about her.

Petey
by Tobi Tobias
New York: G.P. Putnam's Sons, 1978

Petey is Emily's pet gerbil. He faithfully waits in his cage for Emily to come home from school everyday. When Petey becomes ill, Emily and her dad discuss the fact that death is almost certain. Emily's father prepares her for what may happen and encourages her to dwell on her happy memories rather then the seemingly bleak future. When Petey finally dies, Emily compares her grief to the feeling of being hit in the stomach by a rock. She says that every time she looks in the empty cage, she feels empty, too. Emily's mother suggests that in time, Emily may want another gerbil. Emily says that it will never be the same. Her mother's response is, "I never said it would be the same. It can be different, Em, and still be good." Though Emily doesn't completely agree, she says she will think it over and let her mother know.

The Saddest Time
by Norma Simon
Niles, Illinois: Albert Whitman, 1986

This book recounts three situations in which people die and are mourned. The first deals with a young boy named Michael who is told that his Uncle Joe is dying. Michael visits his sick uncle and is unsure of what to say to him. After Uncle Joe dies, Michael attends the family gathering. Michael finds comfort in helping other family members cope with their grief as well. The second account is about a group of students who deal with the death of their classmate, Teddy. Teddy was hit by a car while riding his bicycle. The class decides to write letters to Teddy's parents and tell them about their happy memories of Teddy. The third story is about the death of Emily's grandma. Several years after the death, Emily still misses her grandma, but carries on the tradition of baking oatmeal cookies as she did when her grandma was alive. Each time she eats a cookie, she remembers her grandma with special love.

The Tenth Good Thing About Barney

by Judith Viorst

New York: Atheneum, 1971

A young boy mourns the death of his cat, Barney. His mother suggests that he think of ten good things about Barney to tell his friends at the cat's funeral. At the time of the ceremony, the little boy can only think of nine good things about Barney. It is later, when the little boy is helping his father plant some seeds, that he thinks of the tenth—in death, his cat will nourish new life. The story helps children realize that all living things have a beginning and an eventual end. Children may be inspired by this little boy's example to think of ten good things about the pet or person they love that has died as well.

Why Did Grandpa Die?

by Barbara Shook Hazen

New York: Golden, 1985

Molly has a lot in common with her grandfather. They both have dimples and like pink lemonade. One day, when Molly finds a dead butterfly, she asks her grandfather why it is not moving. He explains that it will never move or fly again because it is dead. Then together they bury the butterfly. The next day Molly's grandfather is taken to the hospital with chest pains and he dies. Molly experiences a variety of emotions as she moves through the grieving process. As time passes, Molly's feelings grow less painful. This is an excellent book about death and grieving. Euphemisms are not used. The story ends by reminding the reader that storytelling is a means of holding onto and passing on family traditions.

Support Groups

It can be very beneficial to enlist the services of support and self-help groups when dealing with grief. There are a number of resources available for this purpose. Consider contacting your local Social Services Department, American Red Cross, County Medical Association, or the United Way. Remember also that clergy and local hospitals and libraries can offer information and assistance. To locate specific support or bereavement groups in your area, call the organizations below for local contacts and phone numbers.

Association of Death Education and Counseling (ADEC)
638 Prospect Avenue
Hartford, Connecticut 06105
This organization is devoted to promoting effective death education and death-related counseling. It distributes educational materials and programs.

Candlelighters Childhood Cancer Foundation
1901 Pennsylvania Ave. NW, Suite 1001
Washington, D.C. 20006
This is an international support network of parents of children who have or have had cancer.

Children in Hospitals
31 Wilshire Park
Needham, Massachusetts 02192
A resource for parents, educators, and health professionals who seek to minimize the trauma of a child's hospitalization.

Compassionate Friends
P.O. Box 1347
Oak Brook, Illinois 60521
For parents who have experienced the death of a child from any cause at any age.

Dougy Center

3090 S.E. 52nd
Portland, Oregon 97206
  A nonprofit center with nationwide affiliates for grieving children who have lost a parent or sibling.

Elisabeth Kübler-Ross Center

South Route 616
Head Waters, Virginia 24442
  This noted expert in death and dying has established a non-profit organization to promote the concept of unconditional love. The center provides educational services and audio-visual materials.

Foundation of Thanatology

630 W. 168 Street
New York, New York 10032
  Presents conferences and publications about bereavement and care for the dying.

Mothers Against Drunk Drivers (MADD)

669 Airport Freeway, Suite 310
Hurst, Texas 76053
  Some chapters offer group support for victims of drunk driving.

National AIDS Hotline

American Social Health Association
P.O. Box 13827
Research Triangle Park, North Carolina 27709
1-800-342-AIDS
  This organization provides recorded information, 24-hours a day, along with referrals to medical centers and free literature.

National Self-Help Clearinghouse

33 W. 42nd Street
New York, New York 10036
  For information on support groups, send a letter describing your circumstances with a self-addressed stamped envelope.

Sudden Infant Death Syndrome (SIDS) Alliance
10500 Little Patuxent Parkway, #420
Columbia, Maryland 21044
  This groups offers services to families who have lost a child to SIDS and provides education and research in the field.

Parents Without Partners, Inc.
8807 Colesville Road
Silver Spring, Maryland 20910
  This organization offers services to single parents and their children to aid in crisis intervention and education.

Index